COUNTRY
BEDROOMS

Fiona Broadwood

A LUMO PUBLISHING BOOK

First published in the UK in 2008

Design Copyright © Fiona Broadwood 2008

Photography and Layout Copyright © Fiona Broadwood 2008

A catalogue record for this book is available from the British Library

ISBN 978-0-9555344-2-3

Photography by Fiona Broadwood & Chloe (Mo) Broadwood

Book Design by Fiona Broadwood & Lucy Broadwood

The projects in this book **<u>are not</u>** suitable for children and are undertaken at your own risk.

The diagrams in this book are not drawn to scale and are included for information and reference purposes only.

<u>Please note</u>

Measurements: Depending how accurate your marking and cutting out both are, some card measurements/lengths may have to be trimmed to fit precisely.

For my daughters,

Lucy & Mo

...the best miniatures I have ever made.

contents...

Introduction...

foreword...   1
welcome to 1:24th Scale...   2
tools...   3
materials...   4
paint...   5
paint techniques...   7

Room Features...

a bedroom fireplace...   9
cupboard staircase (landing)...   15

The Master Bedroom...

a double bed...   19
'lit' Bedside tables...   24
the dressing table & stool...   27
a wardrobe...   30

A Child's Bedroom

a single bed...   34
toy box (open)...   37
a chest of drawers...   39
wall mirror...   41

The room boxes...

master bedroom room box...   43
child's bedroom room box...   45
landing room box...   46
floorboards...   47
rough rendered walls...   49
ceiling beams...   50
cottage latch door...   51
cottage windows...   53

Petite Properties...

petite properties...   55
about the author...   56
also in this series / tile cut outs...   57
acknowledgements...   60

"Introduction..."

foreword...

Dear Reader

As a professional dolls house builder I have always preferred to work in the 1:24th scale, as I have found architectural details can be accurately achieved without difficulty.

Contrary to popular belief, it is incredibly easy to create and build in this smaller scale, with furniture and room features being no exception.

Houses, cottages or shops can be filled with handmade furniture and accessories at very little cost.

In my (humble) opinion 1:24 is fast becoming the ultimate D.I.Y scale and as such it is easy to see why it is rapidly growing in popularity.

Lack of space? No problem!

If space is at a premium then the 1:24th scale is definitely for you. Half scale doll's houses take up very little space, when compared to their larger 1:12th counterparts. The smaller size also allows miniaturists to collect many individual houses, instead of just one or two.   Street scenes can be recreated and displayed in the space of a simple wall shelf.

If, as an avid miniaturist, you are reluctant to restrict your dolls house ownership to just one architectural period or style of property, then the smaller scale houses are for you...   **as less, can mean more!**

1:24th scale collectors can display, many different houses, cottages or shops in the same space that is needed to accommodate just <u>one</u> 12th scale dolls house.

As a result of my work I am constantly asked by my customers where they can find realistic furniture and accessories for their Petite Properties' cottages and also, how best to decorate their 24th scale interiors in order to bring them to life?

Quite simply, from now on... this series of books will be my reply.

Fiona Broadwood
(Bea)

welcome to 1:24th scale...

For all readers new to this scale and for those who maybe embarking on their very first 1:24th scale project, I feel that I should begin by clarifying the 'science bit' of working in this wonderful smaller scale.

The ratio or scale - **1:24** translates simply into:

1 foot = ½ an inch

So for example, a measurement of 1 inch x 2 inches given for a 1:24th scale table top, would translate into a 2 foot x 4 foot table top if it were to be made in real life.

It is also worth noting that the 1:24th scale is sometimes referred to as **half inch scale** or **half scale,** as when compared to the larger and more common 1:12th scale, (1 foot = 1 inch) it is quite simply – **half the size.**

<u>Please note:</u> **The measurements in the project methods within this book are all given in inches, where the abbreviation 'in' = inch is used.**

"The aims of this book..."

This book has been written to inspire owners of 1:24th scale dolls houses to create imaginative country bedrooms, filled with realistic furniture and traditional features. With the aid of step-by-step instructions, combined with easy to understand diagrams and pictures, 1:24th scale cottage interiors can be transformed and brought to life with minimal expense.

Alternatively the upstairs rooms featured in this book, can be made as individual room boxes, an ideal introduction for anyone new to the 1:24th scale.

"No woodwork required..."

Each project in this book has been designed for "mini-makers" of all levels of ability and uniquely **does not** feature the use of hard wood, nor will you require any complicated wood working skills to complete them. Instead, basic art and craft materials are combined with the clever adaptation of every day objects to produce a wide range of cottage furniture and bedroom features.

tools...

When I developed the projects for this book, my main aim was to keep the tools required as simple as possible, you will probably have most of them already.

Many of the 'makes' in fact feature the same tools and materials, just simply utilised in different ways.

Stanley knife or Craft knife: Use whichever knife you feel more comfortable with. I use a combination of the two. For example when I cut mount board which is quite thick, I use a Stanley Knife and for thinner card and more intricate work I use a craft knife or scalpel.

Metal Ruler: After painful mistakes, I strongly recommend you use one with a finger guard and for added safety and accuracy, one with a non slip backing helps to keep the ruler in position whilst cutting.

Pencil: It might sound obvious, but make sure your pencil is well sharpened, as a fine point helps keep measurements precise and accurate.

Bristle brushes: I have always used a widely available children's range of chunky brushes as they are both effective and very economical to use.

Fine paint brushes: I recommend a 'general' selection of water colour brushes. They allow a good quality of finish and are ideal for painting many of the projects in this book.

Garden secateurs: I have found these to be the most easy and effective way to cut toothpicks!

Scissors: Small and large craft scissors. Curved nail scissors are also helpful when cutting out rounded shapes.

Elastic bands: Various sizes for holding parts in place when gluing.

Clothes pegs: Are useful to hold glued card together if like me, you run out of hands!

Tweezers: These are ideal for handling and positioning small items such as furniture handles.

Set square: For accurate marking of 90° angles.

Kitchen sponge: Firm and dense sponges are best. They can be cut to the required size.

Cotton buds: To remove and clean away excess glue etc.

Cutting board: A4 size is ideal.

Wire cutters: The smaller, the better.

Compass : A simple one will do!

3

materials...

The following list is an overview of the basic materials required to complete the projects in this book.

Further information is supplied for any special material requirements for individual projects at the beginning of each set of project instructions.

All materials required are readily available from any good art or craft shop, high street stationary store or even from well stocked market stalls.

- Mount card: **2mm thick**
- Foam core board*: **¼ inch thick**
- Medium card: **old greeting cards are ideal for most projects.**
- Thick card – **cereal boxes etc**
- Beads: selection of styles and sizes
- Balsa wood: 'off cuts' are sufficient.
- Paint: emulsion, poster and matt acrylic varieties.
- Varnish: matt finish (optional)
- Soft tissues
- Tissue paper
- Clear plastic or sheet of acetate*

*required if you wish to make the actual room boxes
See **page 43** for further details...

- Masking tape
- Dress making pins
- paper
- x4 plastic 1:24th scale windows*
- x7 grain of wheat lights: **x4 for lamps and x3 for concealed lighting***
- Polystyrene off cuts
- Baby wipes
- Air dry clay or paper clay: **paper clay works well, but any air hardening clay will do.**
- Adhesives: **PVA & tacky glue**
- Permanent felt tip pens
- Masking tape
- Double sided sticky tape

Top tip...
There are now many recycling centres in the U.K, where you can find a treasure trove of materials suitable for the projects in this series of books.

paint...

Paint... Now there's a subject!

In my opinion paint is a very personal thing. Some people like to use acrylics, whilst others are happy to dab on poster paint. Colours are also an individual choice, influenced by personal preference and by the type of project or period of house you are working on. With this in mind I have given examples below of the types of paint that can be used and also the colours that I personally prefer, highlighted in italics. Remember, there are no right or wrong choices, instead simply what works for you.

Poster Paint...

I have used this type of paint in my 'mucky paint' mix and also in many of the other projects in this series of 'how to' books. Poster paints are both cheap and versatile and are also excellent when mixed with matt emulsion to create any desired tone or colour. They can also help to make more expensive paints, go that little bit further. (*Black, yellow, brown and silver*)

Emulsion tester pots...

These are really useful and come in an infinite range of colours. Most 'tester pots' are only available in a matt finish, which can be easily sealed, if required with a single coat of either matt, satin or gloss finish varnish. I particularly like and use the period inspired colour ranges. Although they are initially more expensive to purchase, they contain a much higher level of pigment and in turn will provide excellent coverage. It may also be helpful to note that some period inspired paint ranges offer additional information on their colour charts. This historical information is helpful if you want to be able to select individual colours to recreate and reflect specific period styles or architectural influences. (*Off white, blue and cream*)

Acrylic paints...

I use this paint a lot and have found that it can easily be mixed to create desired shades and tones as required. There are many inexpensive ranges available, offering an extremely wide selection of colours. *(Medium brown, dark brown, black etc. all in a matt finish)*

Satin wood / Egg shell...

I would only recommend this type of paint for painting furniture. It is ideal if you don't want to have to seal your work with varnish after it has been painted. I would also only advise the use of the water based paints in these finishes, as I have found that they not only dry quickly, but also brushes can be easily cleaned with hot soapy water after use. *(Cream and ivory.)*

Varnish...

Technically not a 'paint' I know, but as I have previously mentioned varnish can be used to seal a variety of matt finish paints. I would advise using a water based varnish as they are normally quick drying, easy to use and give excellent even results. Ranges of water based varnishes normally include matt, satin and high gloss finishes.

> **"Homemade paint mixes..."**

'Mucky' paint mix...

This homemade paint mix is used to distress the rough render on the walls in the country bedrooms and landing area. Simply mix together a little brown, yellow and black poster paint then dilute with water until the mixture resembles muddy puddle water. As with all homemade paint mixes the colour is not an exact science, simply whatever shade and colour of 'dirtiness' that works for you. Excess paint can be stored in jam jars, but remember to shake well and stir thoroughly before use.

'Beam' paint mix...

This is a simple water based mix of poster paint. Blend a little medium brown and black poster paint together, then dilute with enough water to make the final paint mix into a translucent solution that will gently 'stain' the wooden beams, rather than 'paint' them.

paint techniques...

The paint techniques used in this book are not complicated to master and there isn't a long list of difficult skills which need to be learnt and perfected. With the exception of good old fashioned painting there is really only one technique to get to grips and it is a really simple one at that - trust me!

"Dry brush distressing..."

Most of the projects in this book involve a certain amount of 'dirtying' in order to give them an 'aged and used' appearance and it is this that makes the finished piece look so effective. 'Dry brush distressing' is the best technique that I have developed for this purpose. To 'dry brush' simply take a completely dry clean brush and load with a tiny amount of paint. Remove the excess paint from the brush using a piece of tissue, until the brush is almost totally dry. Apply the distressing paint in gentle circular movements over the object you wish to 'age'. Paint will then catch onto the edges of details such as drawers and doors and giving a softer, 'lived in' look to furniture and features. Applying the 'dry brush technique over matt paint will give a dirtier finish as the matt paint will absorb more of the distressing colour used.

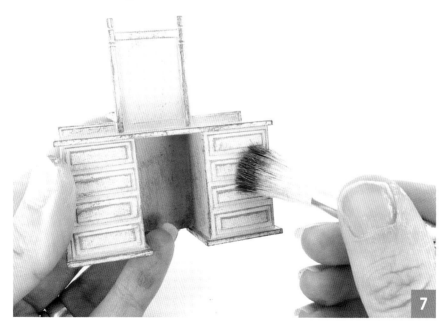

"Room features..."

(Materials listed are required to make both fireplaces...)

Materials...

- ½in thick polystyrene 'off cut'
- Mount board *(2mm thick)*
- Medium Card
- Soft tissues
- Matt emulsion tester pot in chosen room colour
- Black acrylic paint & silver poster paint *(for the black fire surround)*
- Cream & brown acrylic paint *(for the cream fire surround - pictured left)*
- x2 grain of wheat lights (one for each fireplace)
- PVA, tacky glue & double sided sticky tape.
- x2 large paper clips
- x4 dressmaking pins
- x2 tiny seed beads
- Tile 'cut outs' - **see page 57**
- Stickers - optional

Step 1...

Draw out the chimney breast front: **part A** *(see fig. 1)* onto 2mm thick mount board. Cut out using a craft knife and metal ruler. **See picture 1.**

Step 2...

Draw around **part A** onto a piece of ½in thick polystyrene and cut out the polystyrene shape; named **part B** using a craft knife and metal ruler.

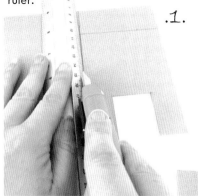

.1.

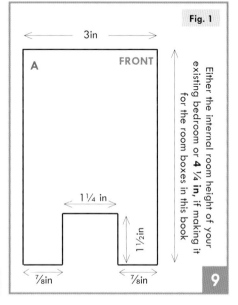

Fig. 1

A   FRONT

3in

1¼ in

1½in

⅞in   ⅞in

Either the internal room height of your existing bedroom or **4 ¼ in**, if making it for the room boxes in this book

Step 3...

.4.

Using PVA adhesive, glue the front; **part A** onto the front on the polystyrene chimney breast; **part B**. Ensure both pieces line up. Weigh down and compress with heavy books or weights if necessary. Leave to dry thoroughly.

Step 4...

.6.

Liberally coat the exterior of the chimney breast in PVA adhesive, then cover with shredded pieces of tissue sheets. Allow the tissue to wrinkle up and crease, as this will add texture to the final wall finish. Patch any areas not covered using small torn sections of tissue, see **picture 4.** Allow to dry completely and harden, ideally leave over night.

Step 5...

Paint the rough rendered chimney breast with 2 coats of matt emulsion. I have used an ivory colour, but any off white, or cream shade would be suitable. Leave to dry completely before continuing to step 6.

Step 6...

Distress the chimney breast using the **dry brush technique:** Take a completely dry, clean brush and load with a small amount of the mucky paint mix. With a dry piece of kitchen paper remove the excess paint from the brush until the bristles are almost dry again. Apply the paint with gentle circular movements, working lightly over the entire chimney breast. The mucky paint will 'catch' upon the rough surface and age the uneven render.

Paint the inside aperture of the chimney breast with 2 coats of black acrylic paint.

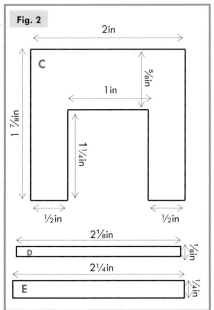

Fig. 2

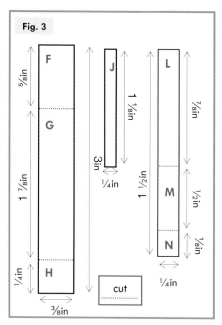

Fig. 3

F

⁵⁄₈in

G

1 ⁷⁄₈in

H

¹⁄₄in

³⁄₈in

J

1 ⅛in

3in

¹⁄₄in

L

⁷⁄₈in

1 ½in

M

½in

N

¹⁄₈in

¹⁄₄in

cut

Step 7...

Draw out the shapes shown in *fig. 2* onto 2mm thick mount board. Cut out using a craft knife and metal ruler. Label with their corresponding letter and set aside.

Step 8...

Draw out the shapes shown in *fig. 3* onto **medium card**. Cut out using a craft knife and metal ruler or scissors if preferred. Cut out x2 each of **parts; F,G,H, L, M and N**.

Label with their corresponding letter and set aside.

Step 9...

Once all the pieces have been cut out, take **part C** and using a little tacky glue, stick on **parts G, G and J** in the positions shown in *fig. 4*, also see **picture 9**.

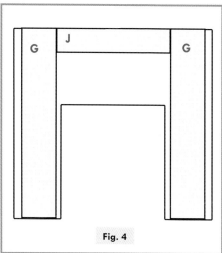

G   J   G

Fig. 4

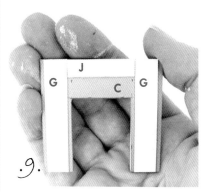

.9.

Step 10...

When dry glue on **parts F, F, L, L, H, H** in the positions shown in *fig. 5*. (See *overleaf*)

Finally glue on **parts M, M, N, N** in the positions shown in *fig.6*. (See *overleaf*) Allow to dry thoroughly.

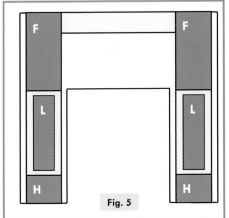

Fig. 5

Step 11...

Next using wire cutters cut a piece of paperclip wire to a length of 1⅛in and glue into position on the fire surround as shown in *fig. 6*, see **picture 11**.

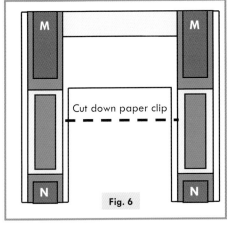

Cut down paper clip

Fig. 6

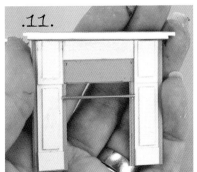

.11.

Step 12...

If preferred, glue a suitable fancy sticker or a 'relief' paper shape onto the front of fire surround to add a textured pattern. Using a little tacky glue, glue **part D and E** on top of each other to form the mantelshelf. Glue the mantle shelf onto the top edge of fire surround, ensuring that the back edge of the shelf is flush with the back of the surround. Leave to dry.

Step 13...

Paint the fire surround with two coats of black or cream acrylic paint.

When dry, distress with a tiny amount of silver poster paint OR brown acrylic paint using the dry brush technique.

See **page 7**. Set aside.

.13.

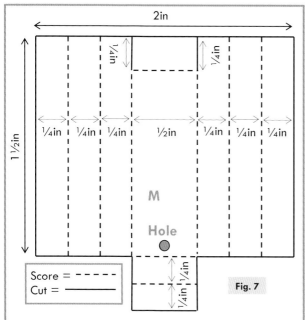

2in

¼in

¼in

1½in

| ¼in | ¼in | ¼in | ½in | ¼in | ¼in | ¼in |

M

Hole

¼in ¼in

¼in ¼in

Score = - - - - -
Cut = —————

Fig. 7

Mark out onto medium card the shape shown in *fig.7*. Score along the appropriate lines and carefully cut out. See **picture 14a.** Next, gently bend the card along the scored lines, as shown in **picture 14b.** This card shape will form the tiled insert of the fireplace and grate.

Step 15...

Using a sharp ended tool, carefully make a hole in **part M** , located as shown in **picture 20** *(See overleaf)* See also *fig. 7*. Ensure that the hole is large enough to allow a bulb from a grain of wheat light to be passed easily through.

.14a.

.14b.

Tiles

Flu flap

Side of grate

Tiles

Side of grate

Side of grate

Grate

Step 16...

Using tacky glue, glue the 2 sides of the grate to the edges of both the grate and the flu flap, see **picture 14b** for identification. Use a peg to hold the fireplace insert in place until the glue is fully dry, see **picture 16.**

Step 17...

Gently push 2 pins through the sides of the grate, from one side to the other, see **picture 17.** *(See overleaf)* Carefully trim the sharp ends off of the pins with wire cutters and se-cure with a dab of tacky glue. Leave to dry. .16.

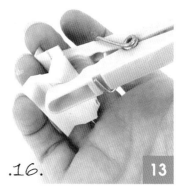

13

.17.

Fire surround shown upside down

Step 18...

Cut a small piece of medium card approximately ⅛in x ⅜in and glue onto the front of the grate to create the illusion of an ash drawer.

Glue a seed bead onto the front of the drawer to form a knob. Allow to dry.

Step 19...

.19.

Paint the fireplace insert; **part M** with 2 coats of black acrylic paint, see **picture 19**. Dry distress with a little silver poster paint using the dry brush technique.

.20.

Step 20...

Cut out the tile strips on **page 57** Cover the back of each strip with double sided sticky tape and stick the tiles onto the front of **part M**, see **picture 14b** for the position. Trim off any excess overlap. Cut another 2 strips of double sided tape and stick onto the rear of **part C**, against the edge of the internal aperture. Stick **part M** onto the back of the fire surround, **part C** ensuring that both parts line up as appropriate, see **picture 20** and finished fireplace picture; *below left.*

Step 21...

Thread the bulb of a grain of wheat light through the hole previously made in **part M**. **Please Note:** When building the room boxes you will need to make additional holes in the walls behind the final location of the fireplace, **see step 5 on page 44.** When ready glue the fireplace permanently into position in the sitting room. Thread the wire of the light through this hole and electrify as per the bulb manufacturer's instructions and advice.

Top tip...

In order to allow for the future replacement of bulbs, it is best not permanently glue the fire surround onto the chimney breast.
Instead hold in place with tacky wax.

Cupboard stairs (landing)...

Materials...

- Soft tissues.
- Mount card (2mm thick)
- ¼ inch thick foam core board (5mm thick board can also be used)
- PVA adhesive & tacky glue
- Mucky paint mix, see pg. 6
- Emulsion paint; tester pot in chosen room colour
- Medium brown acrylic paint
- Black & white poster paint.
- Medium card
- x1 small beads
- Cooking flour
- Grain of wheat light

Step 1...

Draw out **part A** shown in *fig. 8* onto mount board and cut out using a craft knife and metal ruler.

Do not cut out the door shape, instead just mark the door out in pencil, then proceed to **step 2**.

Step 2...

Take **part A** and score along the dotted line marked **'Line A'** shown in *fig.8* (**Do not** *cut all the way through the card*) Next cut out the top, right side and bottom of the door shape marked onto the card, using a craft knife and metal ruler.

Trim the top, right hand side and bottom of the door by about ¹/₁₆ of an inch, as this will allow the door to open and close more easily.

See **picture 2** *(overleaf)*.

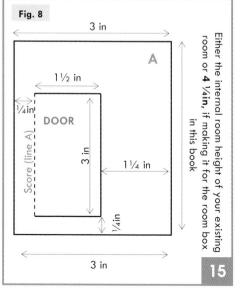

Fig. 8

3 in

1½ in

¼in

DOOR

Score (line A)

3 in

1¼ in

¼in

A

3 in

Either the internal room height of your existing room or 4 ¼in, if making it for the room box in this book

Step 3...

To create the texture on the door; cut irregular strips of medium card. Cut 2 lengths to fit the width of the door and stick one to both the top and bottom. Measure additional strips to fit vertically in between, see **picture 3** and stick onto the door. As the inside of the staircase's door can not be seen, this can be left blank. Allow the glue to dry.

Step 4...

Cut the door surround from a strip of mount card and glue into place using tacky glue, see **step 5 on page 52**.

Step 5...

Paint the door and frame with 2 coats of medium brown acrylic paint. Leave to dry and then distress using the dry brush technique with a little black poster paint. Leave to dry.

Step 6...

Working carefully around the door and frame, cover the outside wall of the cupboard stairs, **part A** with PVA glue. Next cover the glued areas with shredded pieces of tissue. Allow the tissue to wrinkle up and crease as this will add texture to the final wall finish. Patch any areas not covered using small torn sections of tissue. See **picture 6**. Allow to dry completely, ideally leave over night.

Step 7...

When the rendered walls are dry do not become concerned if the mount board has bent out of shape, as the mount card can be easily and gently bent back into place. Paint with 2 coats of paint in your chosen room colour. Leave to dry. Using the dry brush painting technique on page 7 and a little of the mucky paint mix on page 6, gently distress the rough render on **part A**. Finally, glue on a small bead onto the door as a door handle.

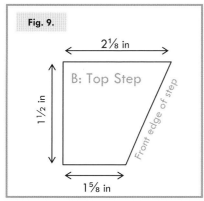

Fig. 9.

B: Top Step

2⅛ in

1½ in

1⅝ in

Front edge of step

.11.

Top tip...

Alternatively, the top step can be made from a piece of ¼ inch thick polystyrene or balsa wood if preferred...

Step 8...

Mark the shape shown in *fig.9.* onto ¼in thick foam core board and cut out using a craft knife and metal ruler.

Step 9...

Using a craft knife, carefully cut out a 'shallow dip' from the front edge of the step to create a worn tread effect.

Step 10...

Cover the top step: **part B** in a liberal quantity of PVA adhesive. Whilst the glue is still wet, cover generously with flour. Set aside and leave to thoroughly dry out and for the glue to harden.

Step 11...

Gently dust off and remove the excess flour. Paint the step with 2 coats of medium grey poster paint. Once completely dry take some dark grey poster paint and gently sponge the paint over the top of the base grey paint, allowing the paint to catch at the edge and tread of the step. See **picture 11.** Leave to dry thoroughly.

Using the dry brush technique and a very tiny amount of black poster paint distress the step.

Step 12...

To fit the cupboard stairs into the landing room box, see **page 46.**

"The master bedroom..."

a double bed...

Materials...

- Mount card (*2mm thick*)
- Foam core board ¼ in thick.
- Medium card
- Cream, white, brown and blue paint (*or your own preferred colours*) in either acrylic paints or tester pots of emulsion paint.
- Tissue paper
- 1 baby wipe - clean and dried.
- x4 Tooth picks (*I have used fancy 'turned' toothpicks for this project*)
- Air dry clay
- Polystyrene off cut; approximately ½in thick
- Selection of blue and green permanent felt tip pens.
- PVA and tacky glue

Step 1...

Draw out a 2¼in x 3in rectangle onto an off cut of ½in thick polystyrene. Cut out using a craft knife and metal ruler.

Next cut a piece of tissue paper approximately 4½in x 5in - this will form the bottom sheet of the bed.

Cover the polystyrene 'mattress' in PVA glue, then lay the tissue sheet over it, allow the tissue to wrinkle up. Glue the edges of the sheet under the mattress. When dry paint with 2 coats of white emulsion. Set aside.

Step 2...

Next draw out **three** 2¼in x 3in rectangles onto ¼in thick foam core board. Cut out using a craft knife and metal ruler. Using PVA glue, stick the three rectangular pieces of foam core board on top of each other in a stack; to form the base of the bed, see **picture 2**. Leave to dry.

Step 3...

Draw out the shapes shown in *fig.10* onto mount board. Label each piece in pencil with the corresponding letter to avoid mistakes during construction. Carefully cut out each shape using a craft knife and metal ruler. **Please note:** cut out x**2** side panels; **part C.**

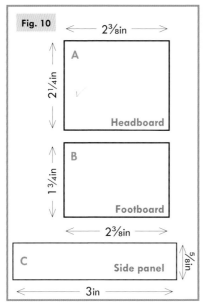

Fig. 10

2³⁄₈in

2¹⁄₄in

A

Headboard

1³⁄₄in

B

Footboard

2³⁄₈in

C Side panel

5⁄₈in

3in

Step 4...

Draw out the shapes shown in *fig.11* onto medium card and label with their corresponding letters, cut out as before.

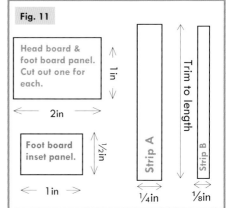

Fig. 11

Head board & foot board panel. Cut out one for each.

1 in

2in

Foot board inset panel.

¹⁄₂in

1 in

Strip A

Trim to length

Strip B

¹⁄₄in

¹⁄₈in

Step 5 ...

Using tacky glue, stick the 2 side panels; **parts C** onto the long edges of the bed base.

When dry glue both the headboard and footboard into position, ensuring that they are at right angles to the bed base, see **picture 5.** Leave to dry.

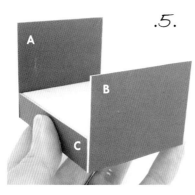

.5.

A

B

C

Step 6 ...

Cut 4 'turned' toothpicks to a length of 1⁷⁄₈in, see **picture 6.** Using tacky glue, stick the trimmed toothpicks into position on the front outside edges of both the head board and the footboard.

See **picture 7.** *(See overleaf)*

Leave to dry.

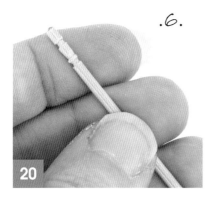

.6.

Step 7...

Cut **strips A and B** to fit between the toothpicks on both the footboard and the headboard and glue into place.

See **picture 7.** *(See overleaf)*

.7.

Step 8...

Next glue on the head and footboard panels, see **picture 8**.

Step 9...

Paint the entire bed in 2 coats of cream acrylic or cream emulsion paint. When dry, distress with a tiny amount of brown acrylic paint using the dry brush technique - see page 7 and **picture 9**

.8.

.9.

Step 10...

Using a selection of permanent felt tip pens in an assortment of blue and green colours; apply tiny areas of clustered dots to create the illusion of a floral painted head and footboard, **see pictures 10a, 10b and 10c.**

Step 11...

Using PVA adhesive, stick the mattress onto the bed base and allow to dry.

.10a.

.10b.

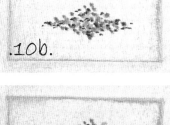

.10c.

Step 12...

To make pillows for the bed simply take a small ball of air dry clay and roll it into a sausage shape approximately ½in in diameter. Cut the clay sausage into x4 1in long sections, see **picture 12a.**

Shape each piece of clay into a 'pillow' shape. Next, using your finger press a dent into the centre of each pillow and bend over the corners as desired, to create 'saggy' looking pillows.

See **picture 12b.** Leave to dry overnight.

.12a.

Step 13...

Cut 8 small squares of tissue paper, which are slightly larger than one side of the pillows. Working on one pillow at a time, take 2 of the tissue paper squares and paint with PVA Adhesive.

Then *(in the style of ravioli pasta)* sandwich the clay pillow in between 2 pieces of tissue paper and press the edges together, also pressing the tissue gently onto the surface of the cushion. See **picture 13**. Always allow the tissue to rumple up and crease as this will add a realistic texture to the finished pillow.

Leave to dry thoroughly in order to allow the PVA to harden the tissue paper.

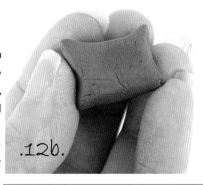

.12b.

Top tip...
Scatter cushions can be made for the bed using the same technique...

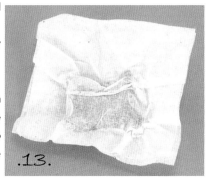

.13.

Step 14...

When completely dry, use scissors to trim away the excess tissue paper from the edges of the pillows, but remember to leave a slight over lap in order to create the frill.

Step 15...

Paint each pillow with 2 coats of white emulsion paint. When dry glue into place onto the bed using a little tacky glue. Leave to dry.

Step 16...

Next cut a rectangle of tissue paper approximately 3in x 3½in and glue to the mattress at the base of the pillows - allow the tissue sheet to cover the pillows so that there is sufficient 'sheet' to fold back over the blanket, see **picture 16.**

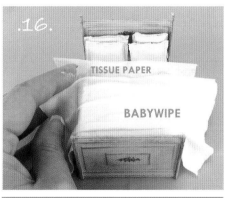

Step 17...

For the bedding, take a clean disposable baby wipe and leave it to completely dry out. Next, cut a small square of the baby wipe fabric approximately 5ins x 2½in. Working on a washable surface, totally coat one side of the baby wipe by painting on PVA adhesive. Carefully lift the baby wipe and 'drape' it over the mattress, see **picture 17.** In order to avoid excess glue marks, ensure that the baby wipe only touches the bed where you want the bedding to permanently drape. Allow the baby wipe to rumple up and fold realistically as

Top tip...
To create a more rumpled and 'slept in' look, screw up the tissue paper into a ball then flattening it back out again before use.

required. Press the baby wipe onto the mattress, sides and contours of the bed using a brush generously loaded with more PVA adhesive. Next fold back the tissue paper top sheet and secure with PVA glue - again, allow it to rumple to create an authentic 'slept in' look. Leave to dry until the baby wipe has hardened, and the adhesive has dried 'clear'.

Step 18...

When dry paint the bedding with 2 coats of acrylic or emulsion paint in the colour of your choice. Distress using the dry brush technique and some of the mucky paint mixture on page 6. Leave to dry thoroughly. Carefully paint the top sheet with 2 coats of white emulsion.

'lit' bedside tables...

Materials...

- Cardboard tube from a roll of tissue
- Thick card
- Masking tape
- Disposable kitchen cloth
- Blue acrylic paint or tester pots of emulsion paint (or in your preferred colour scheme)
- Tacky glue
- Selection of permanent felt tip pens (*blue, green*)
- A white 'gel' pen

Materials for the lamp...

- x2 flower beads*
- x2 8mm wooden beads
- x2 10mm brass eyelets
- x2 grain of wheat bulbs

(Materials listed are those required to make 2 bedside tables)

*PLEASE NOTE: flower beads can only be used for this lamp project if the bulbs remain cold or if the lamp is not going to be electrified.
Safety test your lights before continuing: turn them on and leave them for at least 30 minutes. If your bulbs get warm <u>you must use</u> the alternate metal shade option given on page 26

Step 1...

Take a tissue tube and mark a pencil line around it's circumference; 1⅜in up from the end , see **picture 1**. Carefully cut vertically 'up' the tube from the end and then along the pre-marked pencil line. Cut this curved piece of card to a length of approximately 3½in. Discard the off cut.

.1.

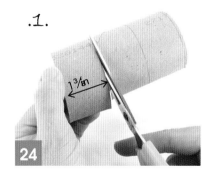

.2.

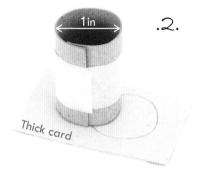

Thick card

.4a.

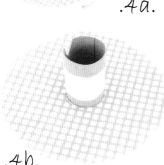

.4b.

Step 2...

Take the curved strip of cardboard and bend it to make a smaller tube approximately 1in in diameter. Fix with a little tacky glue and masking tape. See **picture 2**.

Take an 'off cut' of thick card and draw around one end of the tube. See **picture 2**. Cut out the circle.

Top tip #1...
Curved nail scissors are ideal when cutting out circles.
Top tip #2...
Cereal boxes are a great free source of thick card.

Step 3...

Using a sharp ended tool, carefully make a hole through the circle of thick card. Ensure that the hole is large enough to thread the 2 wires from a grain of wheat bulb and also that the hole is located where you want your lamp positioned on the final bedside table. Stick the card circle onto one end of the small tube and allow to dry.

Step 4...

Using a compass mark out a 4in circle onto a disposable kitchen cloth and cut out, see **pictures 4a and 4b**.

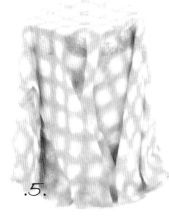

.5.

Step 5...

Working on a washable surface, totally coat one side of the tablecloth with PVA adhesive. Carefully lift the cloth and position in onto the table top and press down, ensuring that the surface is smooth.

Next gently allow the cloth to 'drape' over the table pressing and smoothing the cloth into place using a brush loaded with more PVA adhesive, see **picture 5**.

.6.

Allow the cloth to rumple up and fold realistically as it touches the floor at the base of the table as required. Finally press the cloth securely against the sides of the table. Leave to dry until the cloth has hardened, and the PVA adhesive has dried 'clear'.

Step 6...

Paint the table with 2 coats of blue paint and leave to dry thoroughly. Next, using a dry brush and a tiny amount of a darker shade of blue paint; distress the table, see **picture 6**.

.7a.

Step 7...

Using a white gel pen apply a series of tiny 'squiggles' all over the tablecloth, see **picture 7a**. Next using a selection of permanent felt tip pens in an assortment of blue and green colours; apply tiny areas of clustered dots over the white 'squiggles', see **picture 7b**. Re-puncture the hole in the top of the table. Set aside.

.8a.

.8b.

.7a.

Step 8...

Take the wooden bead and using a tiny amount of tacky glue, stick it into the dip in the top of the brass eyelet. Allow to dry. Next thread the bead and eyelet lamp base onto the wire of a grain of wheat light. Thread the end of the wire through the hole previously made in the tabletop. Thread the wire of the light through this hole, then out from under the table and through a small pilot hole in the back of the room box. The lamp can be fixed in place with a little tacky wax. Electrify as per the bulb manufacturer's instructions and advice.

Top the lamp with either a flower bead or metal filigree bead cap as per the results of the **bulb safety test listed on page 24.**

a dressing table & stool...

Materials...

- Mount card (*2mm thick*)
- Thick, medium & thin card
- Cream, brown, blue (*light & dark shade*) acrylic paint or tester pots of emulsion paint
- Tacky glue & double sided sticky tape
- x8 1mm seed beads (*for the handles*)
- x8 2mm beads (*for the feet*)
- x2 'turned' toothpicks
- Air dry clay
- Tissue paper
- Thin silver foil
- Dark blue permanent felt tip pen

Step 1...

Draw out the shapes shown below in **fig.12** onto a sheet of 2mm thick mount board. Label each piece in pencil with the corresponding letter (as shown below), to avoid mistakes or confusion during construction. Carefully cut out each shape using a craft knife and metal ruler.

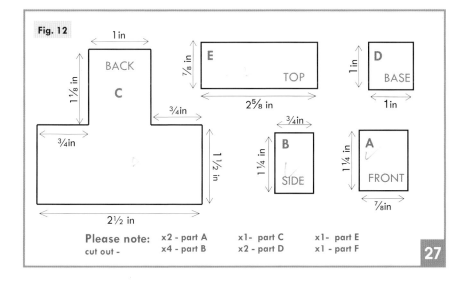

Fig. 12

1 in

1 ⅛ in — BACK

C

¾in

¾in

2½ in

E — ⅞ in

TOP — 2⅝ in

¾in

1¼ in — B — SIDE

1½ in

D — 1in — BASE — 1in

1¼ in — A — FRONT — ⅞in

Please note: cut out -

x2 - part A
x4 - part B

x1- part C
x2 - part D

x1- part E
x1 - part F

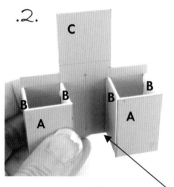

.2.

Step 2...

Using tacky glue, apply glue to the long edges of the 2 sides; **parts B** and stick onto the 2 fronts; **part A** - repeat. See **picture 2**. Clean away excess glue with a cotton bud throughout the construction stages, if required.

Step 3...

Next glue **part C** to the 2 sides; **parts B** to form the back of the dressing table, ensuring that the 2 sides are lined up flush with the bottom of **part C**. See **picture 2**. Leave to dry.

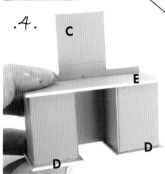

.4.

Step 4...

Using tacky glue, stick on the dressing table's top; **part E** and also the 2 bases; **parts D** onto the top and bottom of the dressing table, see **picture 4**.

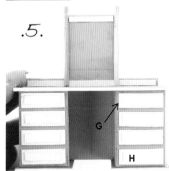

.5.

Step 5 ...

Draw out x8 **part G** and x8 **part H** shown in fig.13 onto medium card, label, cut out and stick into position as shown in **picture 5**.

Step 6...

Take 2 'turned' toothpicks and cut to a length of 1⅜in. Using tacky glue, stick into position onto **part C** as show in **picture 5**. Cut a thin strip of medium card. Cut the strip to fit between the 2 tooth pick at the top and bottom of **part C**, again see **picture 5**. Leave to dry.

.7.

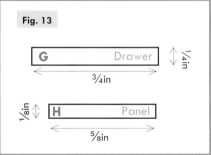

Fig. 13

G	Drawer	↕ ¼in

¾in

⅛in ↕ | H | Panel |

⅝in

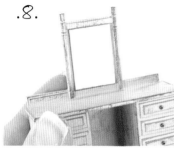

.8.

.9.

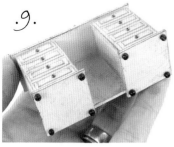

Fig. 14

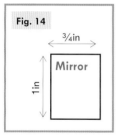

¾in

Mirror

1in

Step 7 ...

Paint the dressing table in 2 coats of cream acrylic paint. When dry, distress with a tiny amount of brown acrylic paint using the dry brush technique, see **picture 7.**

Step 8 ...

Onto medium card mark out the shape show in *fig14* and cut out. Cover the card in double sided tape and carefully stick on some thin silver foil, or silver leaf. Trim away any excess from the edges. Glue the mirror into place, see **picture 8.**

Step 9...

Using tiny dabs of tacky glue, glue the 8 tiny seed beads onto the drawer fronts to create handles. Next glue the x8 2mm beads onto the base of the dressing table to form the feet. Leave to dry.

Step 10 ...

To make the stool cut a strip of thin card ¾in wide x 2¼ long. Follow **steps: 2, 4, 5,** and **6** as given for the bedside table on **pages 25** and **26** However, you must instead substitute a 2½in circle of tissue paper in place of the disposable kitchen cloth.

To make the stool's cushion, take a small ball of air dry clay and gently 'flatten' it with your finger so that it fits on top of the stool. When the clay is dry cover with tissue paper. Paint in the same way as the bedroom stool. Using a dark blue permanent felt tip pen add 2 rows of tiny dots around the top of the cushion and around the top of the stool to create a 'piping' effect. Glue the cushion into place on top of the stool using a little tacky glue.

a wardrobe...

Materials...

- 2mm mount board
- Medium card
- Cream & brown acrylic paint
- Tacky Glue
- x6 1mm beads
  (for the wardrobe's handles)
- x4 2mm beads
  (for the wardrobe's feet)

Step 1...

Draw out the shapes shown below in *fig.15* onto a sheet of 2mm thick mount board. Label each piece in pencil with the corresponding letter (as shown below), to avoid mistakes or confusion during construction.

Carefully cut out each shape using a craft knife and metal ruler.

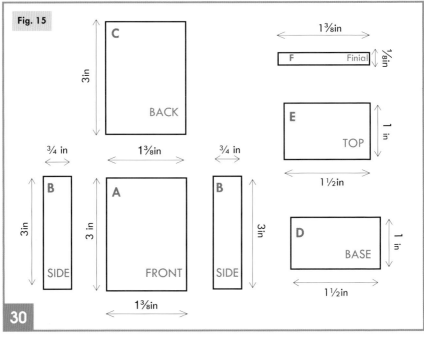

Fig. 15

C — BACK — 3in — 1⅜in

F — Finial — 1⅜in — ⅛in

E — TOP — 1in — 1½in

¾ in — 1⅜in — ¾ in

B — SIDE — 3in

A — FRONT — 3 in — 1⅜in

B — SIDE — 3in

D — BASE — 1in — 1½in

Step 2...

Using tacky glue, glue the long edges of the 2 sides; **parts B** and stick onto the front of the wardrobe; **part A**, see **picture 2**. Clean away excess glue with a cotton bud throughout the construction stages.

Step 3...

Next glue **part C** to the 2 sides; **parts B** to form the back of the wardrobe. See **picture 3**. Allow to dry.

Step 4...

Using tacky glue, glue the top; **part E** and also the base; **part D** onto the top and bottom of the wardrobe, see **picture 4**.

Next glue the finial; **part F** into position on top of **part E**, see **picture 6** (overleaf).

Step 5...

Draw out x2 parts; **G**, **H**, **J** and **K** as shown in fig.16 onto medium card, label and cut out.

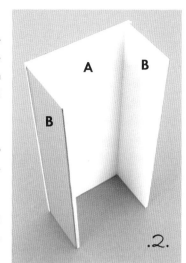

.2.

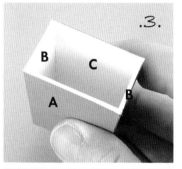

.3.

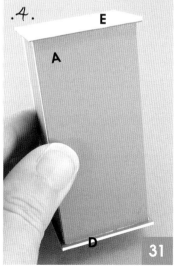

.4.

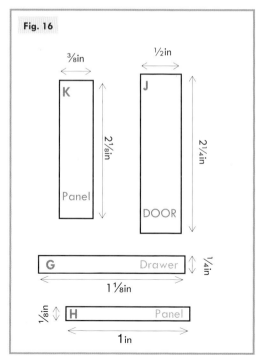

Fig. 16

K — Panel
³⁄₈in, 2⁷⁄₈in

J — DOOR
½in, 2¹⁄₄in

G — Drawer
1¹⁄₈in, ¹⁄₄in

H — Panel
1in, ¹⁄₈in

.6.

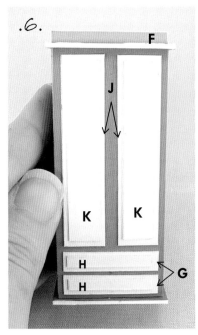

F

J

K   K

H

H

G

Top tip...

Cover the back of the medium card with double sided sticky tape before cutting out the wardrobe's; doors, drawers and panels. Remove the tape's backing and stick into place, to help speed up the gluing process and provide instant adhesion.

Step 6...

Using tacky glue, stick **parts; G, H, J** and **K** into position, as shown in **picture 6.**

Step 7 ...

Paint the wardrobe with 2 coats of cream acrylic paint.

Leave to dry.

Distress with a tiny amount of brown acrylic paint using the dry brush technique.

Step 8 ...

Using tiny dabs of tacky glue, glue the 6 tiny seed beads onto the drawer and door fronts to create handles.

Next glue the x4 2mm beads onto the base of the wardrobe to form the feet.

Leave to dry.

"A child's bedroom..."

a messy single bed...

Materials...

- Mount card (*2mm thick*)
- Foam core board ¼ in thick.
- Medium card
- Dark blue, light & white, paint (*or your own preferred colours*) in either acrylic paints or tester pots of emulsion paint.
- Tissue paper
- 1 baby wipe - clean and dried.
- x2 Tooth picks (*I have used fancy 'turned' toothpicks for this project*)
- Air dry clay
- Polystyrene off cut; approximately ½in thick
- Selection of blue and green permanent felt tip pens
- White gel pen
- PVA and tacky glue

Step 1...

Draw a 1½in x 3in rectangle onto an off cut of ½in thick polystyrene. Cut out using a craft knife and metal ruler. Next cut a piece of tissue paper approximately 3½in x 5in; this will form the bottom sheet of the bed. Cover the polystyrene 'mattress' in PVA glue, then lay the tissue sheet over it, allow the tissue to wrinkle up. Glue the edges of the sheet under the mattress. When dry, paint with 2 coats of white emulsion. Set aside.

Step 2...

Next draw out **two** 1½in x 3in rectangles onto an off cut of ¼in thick foam core board. Cut out using a craft knife and metal ruler. Using PVA glue, stick the two rectangular pieces of foam core board on top of each other; to form the base of the bed. Leave to dry.

Top tip...

Scrunch the tissue paper into a ball before use, in order to give the bed a more 'slept in' look.

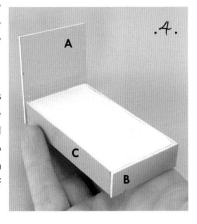

34

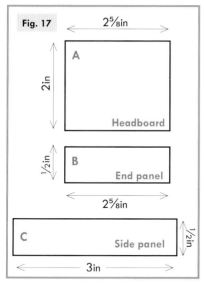

Fig. 17

← 2⅝in →

2in ↕

A

Headboard

½in ↕

B

End panel

← 2⅝in →

C

Side panel

½in ↕

← 3in →

.6.

.7a.

.7b.

Step 3...

Draw out the shapes shown in *fig.17* onto mount board. Carefully cut out each shape using a craft knife and metal ruler. **Please note:** cut out **2** side panels; **part C**.

Step 4...

Using tacky glue, stick the 2 side panels; **parts C** onto the long edges of the bed base and **part B** onto the end of the bed, ensuring the top edges of all of the panels are flush with the surface of the bed base. Leave to dry.

Next glue the headboard into position, ensuring that it is at a right angle to the bed base, see **picture 4**. Leave to dry.

Step 5...

Cut 2 toothpicks to a length of 1⅝in. Using tacky glue, glue into position onto the front outside edges of the headboard. Cut a strip of medium card; approximately ⅛in wide. Measure and cut the strip to fit at the top of the headboard, between the 2 toothpicks.

Step 6...

Paint the bed with 2 coats of dark blue paint. When dry distress using the dry brush technique and a little of the 'mucky paint' mix on page 6.

Step 7...

Using a selection of permanent felt tip pens in an assortment of blue and green colours and a white gel pen; apply tiny areas of clustered dots to create the illusion of a floral painted headboard, see **pictures 7a and 7b**.

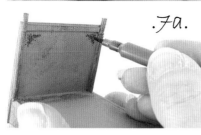

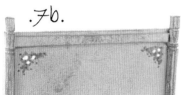

.9.

Step 8...

Using PVA adhesive, stick the mattress onto the bed base and allow to dry.

Step 9...

To make the single bed's pillows, simply follow the instructions previously given in **steps; 12, 13, 14 and 15** on page 22. To create a more 'slept in appearance mould the 2 pillows accordingly, see **picture 9.**

.10a.

.10b.

Step 10...

Next cut a rectangle of tissue paper; 3in x 2½in and a rectangle of baby wipe; 3in x 5in and follow the instructions given in **steps; 16, 17** and **18** on page 23. See also **picture 10a.** To make the bed appear un-made, simply pull both the tissue sheet and baby wipe towards the bottom of the bed and allow to rumple up as appropriate before leaving to dry and harden. See **picture 10b**

a toy box...

Materials...

- 2mm thick mount card
- Medium card
- Medium blue acrylic paint.
- x1 cream 1mm seed bead
- Tacky glue
- Selection of blue and green permanent felt tip pens
- White gel pen

Step 1...

Draw out the shapes shown below in **fig.18** onto 2mm thick mount board. Label each piece in pencil with the corresponding letter (as shown below) Carefully cut out each shape using a craft knife and metal ruler. Score along line A on **part C**.

Step 2...

Using tacky glue, apply glue along the long edges of the 2 sides; **parts B** and stick onto the front of the toy box; **part A**, see **picture 2.** Clean away excess glue with a cotton bud throughout the construction stages.

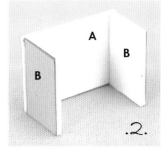

.2.

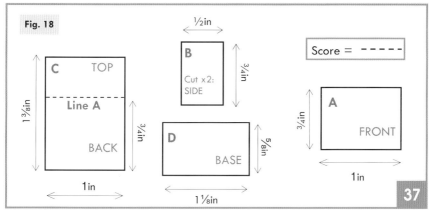

Fig. 18

C — TOP

Line A

BACK

1³⁄₈in

¾in

1in

½in

B

Cut x2: SIDE

¾in

D

BASE

1¹⁄₈in

⁵⁄₈in

Score = - - - - -

¾in

A

FRONT

1in

Step 3...

Next glue the back; **part C** to the 2 sides; **parts B** to form the back of the toy box, ensuring the scored line A is on the exterior of the box. See **picture 3**. Allow to dry.

Step 4...

Using tacky glue, glue the base; **part D** onto the bottom of the toy box, ensuring that the back of the base is flush with the back of the toy box, see **picture 4**.

Step 5 ...

Draw out panels; **parts; E** and **F** as shown in *fig.19* onto medium card and cut out. Glue into position onto the lid and front of the toy box as shown in **pictures 3** and **4**. Next cut a thin strip of medium card approximately ⅛in wide x 2¼in long; **part G** and glue it onto the sides and front edge of the lid. See **pictures 3** and **4**. Leave to dry.

Step 6 ...

Paint the toy box with 2 coats of medium blue paint, see **picture 6**. When dry distress using the dry brush technique and a little of the 'mucky paint' mix on page 6.

Step 7...

Using a selection of permanent felt tip pens in an assortment of blue and green colours and a white gel pen; apply tiny areas of clustered dots to create the illusion of floral painted panels to the lid and front.
see **picture 7**.

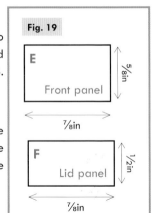

Fig. 19

E — Front panel — ⅝in — ⅞in

F — Lid panel — ½in — ⅞in

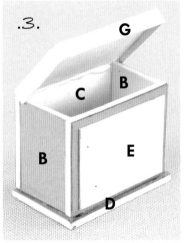

.3.

G

C B

B E

D

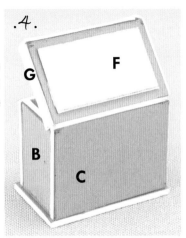

.4.

G F

B C

.6.

.7.

chest of drawers...

Materials...

- 2mm mount board
- Medium card
- Cream & brown acrylic paint
- Tacky Glue
- x12 1mm beads
  (for the chest of drawer's handles)
- x4 2mm beads
  (for the chest of drawer's feet)

Step 1...

Draw out the shapes shown below in **fig.20** onto a sheet of 2mm thick mount board. Label each piece in pencil with the corresponding letter (as shown below), to avoid mistakes or confusion during construction. Carefully cut out each shape using a craft knife and metal ruler.

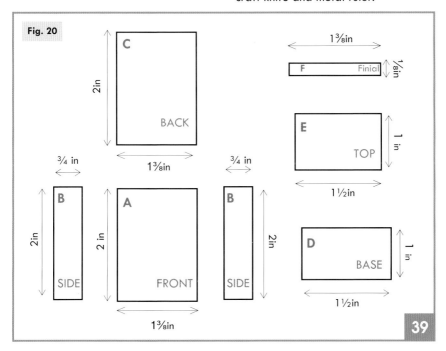

Fig. 20

C — BACK — 2in × 1⅜in

F — Finial — 1⅜in × ⅛in

E — TOP — 1in × 1½in

¾ in   ¾ in

B — SIDE — 2in
A — FRONT — 2in × 1⅜in
B — SIDE — 2in

D — BASE — 1in × 1½in

Step 2...

Using tacky glue, glue the long edges of the 2 sides; **parts B** and stick onto the front of the chest of drawers; **part A.** Clean away excess glue with a cotton bud throughout the construction stages.

Step 3...

Next glue **part C** to the 2 sides; **parts B** to form the back of the chest of drawers.   See **picture 3**. Allow to dry.

Step 4...

Using tacky glue, glue the top; **part E** and also the base; **part D** onto the top and bottom of the chest of drawers, see **picture 4**.

Next glue the finial; **part F** into position on top of **part E**, see **picture 5**.

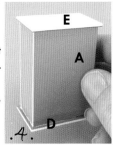

Step 5 ...

Draw out x2 **parts; G, H, L** and **M** and x4 **parts; J** and **K** as shown in *fig.21* onto medium card, label and cut out.   Glue onto the front of the chest of draws in the positions shown in **picture 5.**

Step 6 ...

Paint the chest of drawers with 2 coats of cream acrylic paint. Leave to dry.

Distress with a tiny amount of brown acrylic paint using the dry brush technique.

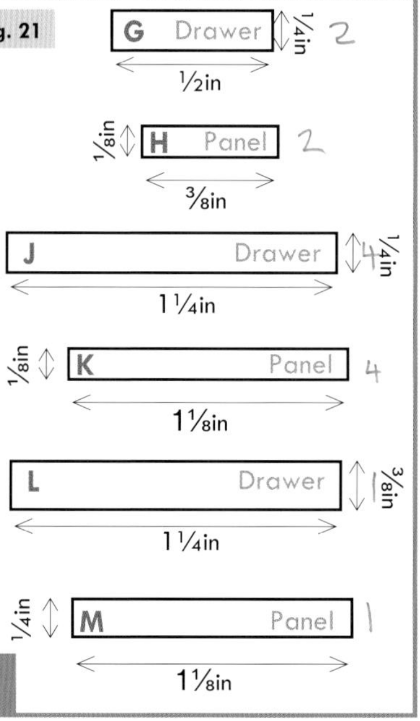

Step 7 ...

Using tiny dabs of tacky glue, glue the 12 tiny seed beads onto the drawer and door fronts to create handles.

Next glue the x4 2mm beads onto the base of the wardrobe to form the feet.

Fig. 21

G Drawer	¼in 2
½in	
H Panel	2
⅛in ⅜in	
J Drawer	¼in
1¼in	
K Panel	4
⅛in 1⅛in	
L Drawer	⅜in
1¼in	
M Panel	1
¼in 1⅛in	

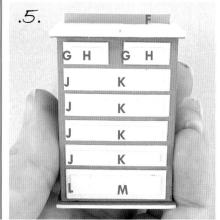

.5.

G H	G H
J	K
J	K
J	K
J	K
L	M

F

a wall mirror...

Materials...

- Mount card
- Medium brown & black acrylic paint
- x4 turned toothpicks
- Thin silver foil
- Double sided sticky tape
- Tacky glue

Step 1...

Onto mount board, draw out a 1½in x 1in rectangle and cut out using a craft knife and metal ruler.

Step 2...

Cut 2 toothpicks, each to a length of 1¼in. Using tacky glue, stick the toothpicks into position on either side of the front of the mirror, see **picture 2**.

Step 3...

Cut another 2 toothpicks, each to a length of approximately 1in. Joining them in the middle, see **picture 3**, stick into position onto the top edge of the mount card. Cut 2 thin strips of medium card to

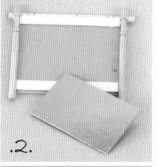

.2.

fit between the 2 toothpicks on the front top and bottom of the mirror surround. See **picture 2**. Paint with 2 coats of medium brown

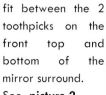

Back view

.3.

acrylic paint and distress using the dry brush technique with a little black paint.

Step 4...

Cut a 1¼in x ¾in rectangle of medium card and cover with double sided tape. Carefully stick on some thin silver foil. Trim away any excess from the edges, glue the mirror into place.

"the room boxes..."

the master bedroom...

Materials...

- Foam core board*
  (¼in thick)
- x2 - 6 pane plastic windows
  (see pg. 53)
- PVA adhesive
- Dressmaker's pins (optional)
- Masking tape (optional)

*6mm thick wooden MDF board can
be used if desired, please follow
manufacturer health and safety
instructions when cutting & sanding..

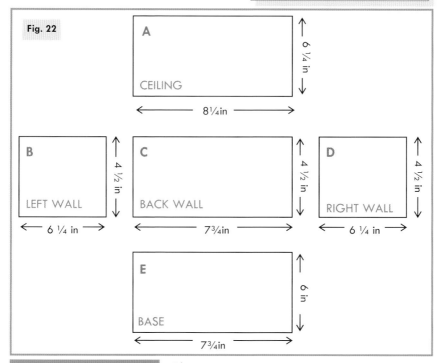

Fig. 22

A — CEILING — 6¼ in — 8¼in

B — LEFT WALL — 4½ in — 6¼ in

C — BACK WALL — 4½ in — 7¾in

D — RIGHT WALL — 4½ in — 6¼ in

E — BASE — 6 in — 7¾in

Top tip...

**3mm thick card can be
used. Simply stick 2 sheets
together using a liberal
even coat of PVA adhesive.
Allow to dry completely,
ensuring that the card sheet
remains flat...**

Step 1...

Mark out **parts A, B, C, D** and **E** shown above in
fig. 22 onto ¼ inch thick foam core board and cut
out carefully using a craft knife and metal ruler.
Please note: if you are using thinner card, the
measurements given above will have to be
adjusted accordingly.

43

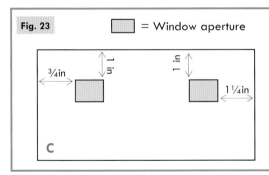

Fig. 23   ▭ = Window aperture

¾in   1 in   1 in   1¼in

C

Step 2...

At this point please follow instructions for the floorboard project, **see page 47.**
Once complete, continue onto step 3.

Step 3...

Follow and complete the window instructions on **page 53.** Next, draw around the completed window onto **part C,** positioning the window apertures as shown in **fig.23.** However these positions are only given as an approximate guide and can be modified to suit your own personal layout or scheme. Using a craft knife and metal ruler cut out an aperture that is approximately ⅛ inch **smaller** than the outline previously drawn onto **part C.** This will allow the window to be glued onto the 'outside' of the room box, on the back of the rear elevation, when the room box is completed.

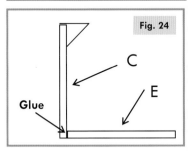

Top tip 1...
Hold room box joins together with masking tape whilst they are drying...

Top tip 2...
Dress making pins can be pushed into the wall joins from the outside of the box to help strengthen the room box...

Step 4...

To complete the room box's rough rendered walls please see **page 49.** Once complete continue onto **step 5.**

Step 5...

Using PVA adhesive, glue the back wall; **part C** at right angles to the back edge of the base; **part E,** see **fig. 24.** Allow to dry.

Step 6...

Glue on side walls; **parts B** and **D** onto each end. Allow to dry. Remember to make pilot holes for the hidden lighting; behind the fireplace and also behind the final position of each of the bedside tables.

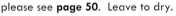

Fig. 24

C

E

Glue

Step 7...

Stick the latch door and chimney breast into position. Glue the ceiling; **part A** onto the top of the room box, fill and touch up the wall joins. Fit ceiling beam into place, please see **page 50.** Leave to dry.

a child's bedroom...

Materials...

- Foam core board* (¼in thick)
- x1 - 6 pane plastic windows (see pg. 53)
- PVA adhesive
- Dressmaker's pins (optional)
- Masking tape (optional)

6mm thick wooden MDF board can be used if desired, please follow manufacturer health and safety instructions when cutting & sanding..

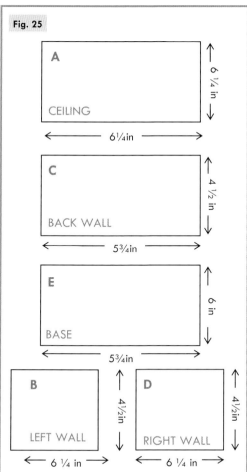

Fig. 25

A

CEILING

6 ¼ in

6¼in

C

BACK WALL

4 ½ in

5¾in

E

BASE

6 in

5¾in

B

LEFT WALL

4½in

6 ¼ in

D

RIGHT WALL

4½in

6 ¼ in

Step 1...

Mark out **parts A, B, C, D** and **E** shown above in *fig. 25* onto ¼ inch thick foam core board and cut out carefully using a craft knife and metal ruler. Then follow steps 2 to 7 on **page 44.**

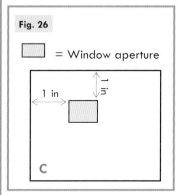

Fig. 26

= Window aperture

1 in

1 in

C

45

a cottage landing...

Materials...

- Foam core board* (¼in thick)
- PVA adhesive
- Dressmaker's pins (optional)
- Masking tape (optional)

*6mm thick wooden MDF board can be used if desired, please follow manufacturer health and safety instructions when cutting & sanding..

Step 1...

Mark out **parts A, B, C, D** and **E** shown in **fig. 27** onto ¼ inch thick foam core board and cut out carefully using a craft knife and metal ruler. Paint the back 1½in of the base: **part E** *(the inside of the cupboard staircase)* with the same grey paint effects as previously used for the top step, see **page 16** and **picture 1**.

After completing the cupboard stairs (landing) project on **pages 15, 16 and 17**, continue **to step 2.**

.1.

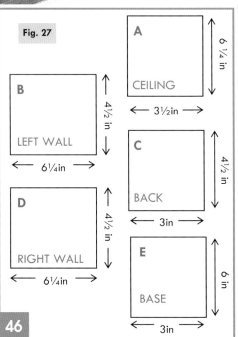

Step 2...

Stick the false top step into position onto the base ; **part E**, see **picture 1.**

Step 3...

Follow **steps 2, 4, 5, 6** and **7** on **page 44.** When completing **step 6** remember to stick the landing's partition wall and doorway into place before continuing, see **picture 3.**

Fig. 27

A

CEILING

← 3½in →

6¼in

B

LEFT WALL

← 6¼in →

4½ in

C

BACK

← 3in →

4½ in

D

RIGHT WALL

← 6¼in →

4½ in

E

BASE

← 3in →

6 in

.3.

floorboards...

Step 1...

Take a piece of medium card which is slightly wider and longer than the floor area that you wish to board. Using a chunky bristle brush paint the whole of one side of the card with one coat of burnt umber acrylic paint, ensuring that your brush strokes stay in one direction, see **picture 1**.
Leave to dry thoroughly

Step 2...

Using a clean dry chunky bristle brush apply small amounts of medium brown paint to the card, again working in 'lines' moving the brush lightly across the surface in the same direction.
See **picture 2**. Leave to dry.

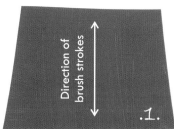

Direction of brush strokes

.1.

Step 3...

Using a clean dry chunky bristle brush repeat step 3, this time using black paint, see **picture 3**.
Leave to dry.

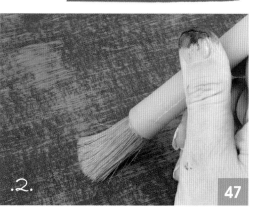

.2.

Step 4...

Using either a craft knife and metal ruler or a guillotine, cut the card into strips. The 'floorboards' should be *(approximately)* either ⅛in, ¼in and ½in wide.

Please note: Ensure that the strips are cut in the same direction as the previous brush strokes.

Step 5...

Paint the floor of the room box with one coat of black acrylic paint and allow to dry before continuing.

Step 6...

Working on a small strip of floor at a time, spread PVA glue onto the base **part E** and then stick on the floorboard strips leaving tiny gaps between each one. Ensure that all the edges and each end of the boards are securely stuck down. Occasionally cut a floorboard in 2 to recreate a planked effect to the floor and to add a feeling of 'age and realism', see **picture 6**.

Step 7...

Once the whole floor has been covered with floorboards, leave to dry thoroughly before trimming away the excess.

See **picture 7**.

N.B If you are floor boarding a pre built dolls house cut a piece of mount card that is an exact fit of the existing floor.

Glue the floorboards to the mount card template, then glue the false floor into place inside the room.

rough rendered walls...

Materials...

- PVA adhesive
- Tissues
- Polystyrene
- Matt emulsion: tester pot in chosen room colour
- 'Mucky' paint mix: See *page. 6*

Step 1...

Cut a strip of polystyrene at a 45° angle and stick onto the top of all 3 of the room box backs: **part C** to create the illusion of the beginning of the 'eves' along the top of the rear bedroom wall, see **picture 1**.

.1.

.3.

Step 2...

First draw round false doors or around anything that is to be attached to the wall, such as the cupboard stairs, latch doors or chimney breasts.

Do not apply render to these marked out areas or areas where two parts of the room box need to be joined together, otherwise the doors, walls etc will not adhere flush against the wall when they are glued in place once the render process has been finished.

Step 3...

Liberally coat the walls with PVA adhesive, then cover with shredded pieces of tissue sheets. Allow the tissue to wrinkle up and crease, as this will add texture to the final wall finish. Allow to dry completely, ideally leave over night.

.3.

Top tip...

If your walls warp slightly during the drying process, simply lay them onto a flat surface and weigh them down under heavy books. Leave the walls to flatten, ideally over night.

Step 4...

Paint the rough rendered walls with two coats of matt emulsion. Leave to dry completely before distressing with a little 'mucky paint' using the dry brush technique on page 7.

ceiling beams ...

Materials...

- Length of balsa wood
- 'Beam paint' mix -
  see page. 6
- Black poster paint
- Tacky glue

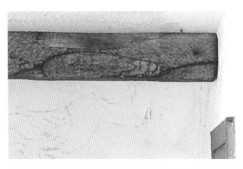

Step 1...

Cut a length of balsa wood to the measurements provided in **fig. 28**. *(or the measurement of your room if not completing the room box projects in this book)*

Fig. 28

Room width

5/8 in

1/2 in

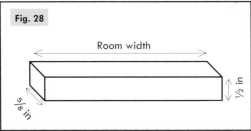

Step 2...

Using a craft knife, cut away and round the edges of the beam. Add notches, holes and cuts to age the wood's appearance, **see picture 2**.

Step 3...

Apply 1 coat of the 'beam paint' mix, see page 6. Allow to dry completely.

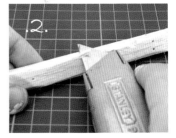

Step 4...

Distress the ceiling beam with a tiny amount of black poster paint, using the dry brush technique. When dry glue the beam onto the ceiling using tacky glue.

Top tip... **alternatively to create a 'seaside' cottage feel simply paint the beams with a white 'wash' of emulsion and when dry, distress with the dry brush technique, using a little of the mucky paint mix...**

cottage latch door...

Materials...

- Mount board
- Medium card
- Medium brown acrylic paint
- Black poster paint
- Small length of garden wire
- x2 pins.
- Black permanent marker pen
- Tacky glue
- Double sided sticky tape

False doors are an easy and effective way to give the illusion of depth within a room. They also help to give a property the illusion of depth, of further rooms and can also hint at hidden unseen areas...

Step 1...

Onto medium card, mark and cut out the main door shape, as shown in *fig.29*.

Step 2...

Cut multiple lengths of medium card to represent the irregular planking strips on the front of the cottage door. Using tacky glue stick each length of card onto the door template, see **picture 2a**. Next cut to fit and glue on 3 horizontal card 'planks' and 2 diagonal planks. See **picture 2b**. Leave to dry.

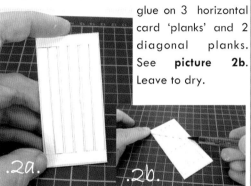

.2a.   .2b.

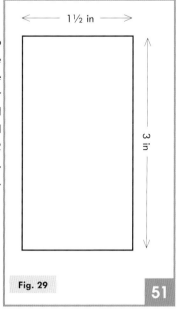

←——— 1½ in ———→

3 in

Fig. 29

Step 3...

Paint the door with 2 coats of medium brown acrylic paint. See **picture 3**. Leave to dry thoroughly.

Step 4...

Using a tiny amount of black poster paint, distress the door using the dry brush technique. See **picture 4**.

Step 5...

From mount card cut a strip approximately ¼ inch wide by 10 inches long. Mark 45°angles and cut the strip into 3 pieces as shown in **picture 5**, so that it fits snugly around the edges of the false door to create a simple door frame. Paint; repeating steps 3 and 4.

Step 6...

Place the door onto something soft (I used a spare piece of balsa wood) and gently hammer a dress maker's pin into the area of the door where your want the latch located. Repeat and make a second tiny pin hole next to the first. See **picture 6**.

Step 7...

Using a permanent black marker pen, colour in the two pin heads.

Step 8...

Push the 2 pins into the holes in the door. With wire cutters, trim away the excess protruding length of the pins from the back of the door. Fix the pinheads in place with a little dab of tacky glue onto the holes on the back of the door.

Step 9...

Cut a tiny length of garden wire and curve one end. Again using permanent black marker pen, colour in. When dry glue into place, laying the wire across the top of the 2 pin heads, see **picture 9**.

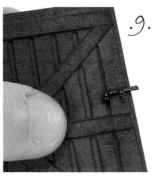

Step 10...

Fix the false door into position using double sided sticky tape. Next glue the door frame around the door with tacky glue.

cottage windows...

Materials...
- x3 6 pane 1:24th scale plastic windows
- Medium brown & black acrylic paint
- Clear acetate

Step 1...
Take x3 plastic 6 pane windows, see **picture below** and remove the inset panes.

Step 2...
The windows can be primed using an aerosol matt primer if required. Remember to spray both sides of the window panes thoroughly, following the paint manufacturer's health and safety instructions. Leave to dry.

Windows can then be painted with acrylic paint or by using a suitable aerosol spray paint. Whatever paint type you choose, apply 2 coats, allowing the windows to dry completely between each application.

To glaze cut a small piece of clear plastic large enough to fit between the front and rear window panes. Reconstruct the windows.

Step 3...
Windows can be distressed and aged using the dry brush technique and a little black acrylic paint. Distressing the window panes **<u>after</u>** they are glazed allows the windows to become dirty and in turn partially obscured too.

53

"Petite Properties..."

petite properties...

As a 1:24th scale dolls house builder I have made hundreds of different properties. Each of my houses, cottages or shops are different and lovingly handcrafted as 'one off' creations.

My 'Country Town Collection' features an ever growing selection of period inspired properties and allows miniaturists to collect, display, fill and enjoy their very own personal and nostalgic street scenes.

"authentic architecture in miniature..."

Each Petite Property is specifically designed to a standardized depth, to allow each one to be displayed side by side to recreate traditional street scenes that celebrate the best in British architecture and heritage.

All Petite Properties feature an exclusive and realistic external finish, whilst the interiors are left as a blank canvas to allow their new owners to express their own creativity and imagination.

1:24th scale dolls houses available from £49.99

www.petite-properties.com

about the author...

Growing up I always harboured the urge to create. Throughout my childhood and teenage years, my Mum always nurtured my creativity and made sure that I was provided with a constant supply of cereal boxes, toilet rolls, yoghurt pots and most importantly, **inspiration!**

In fact, looking back at my childhood, I can't really remember a time when I didn't have my head stuck in a cardboard box, engrossed in gluing, cutting or painting and completely lost in my very own imaginary world.

One memorable Christmas morning I woke to find my stocking filled with lots of little knobbly parcels. On opening, they turned out to be little, simple pieces of wooden furniture. I was ecstatic and my mind immediately began to race with ideas for the type of wonderful 'box' house I could create to put them in.

Of course, downstairs waiting for me under the tree, was a wonderful 1970's style house complete with four open plan rooms and best of all: two real working lights.

To be truthful I can't remember anything else about that Christmas, just that I spent all of it moving furniture around and looking through the windows, finally understanding what it would be like to be a giant.

Unfortunately for my parents, it did not take me long to decide that my new dolls house needed some remodelling. Several cardboard modifications later and I had proudly transformed my house with extra partitions, secret doorways and not forgetting a new single storey 'shoe box' extension, which I had proudly and somewhat permanently glued on.

To this day, I whole heartedly believe it was at this very instance that the complete concept of **PETITE PROPERTIES** first sparked into life and the seed was sown deep inside my imagination. Now, some 25 years later... here I am!

Then...

...and now!

56

A COUNTRY KITCHEN

...bringing 1:24th scale to life

By
Fiona Broadwood

£8.99

A COUNTRY SITTING ROOM

...bringing 1:24th scale to life

By
Fiona Broadwood

£8.99

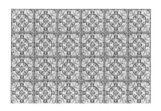

Tile 'cut outs' for
fireplace surrounds

acknowledgements...

My love and thanks as always to...

My husband Tony;
For his gift of self belief...

Lucy, for always knowing when I need a hug.

Mo, (Chloe) for making me laugh and smile, everyday.

I would also like to thank...

Jackson's Miniatures
for their kind permission to use their window in this book.

Please note: The 1:24th windows used in this project are available to purchase online from Petite Properties Ltd
www.petite-properties.com

The Dolls' House Magazine, Guild Of Master Craftsman, Anthony Bailey - for permission to use their front cover image of: **Issue 94.**
featuring:
Fiona Broadwood of Petite Properties